FIVE SECRETS
OF LIVING

P9-DFF-127

5 secrets of living

by Warren W. Wiersbe

Tyndale House Publishers, Inc.
WHEATON, ILLINOIS

Unless otherwise
noted, the Scriptures
in this book are from
the *New American
Standard Bible.*

Cover photo by
Grant Heilman.
Inside photos by
Robert McKendrick.

Library of Congress
Catalog Card Number
77-083549
ISBN 0-8423-0870-9

Copyright © 1977
Tyndale House
Publishers, Inc.
Wheaton, Illinois.
All rights reserved.
First printing,
February 1978

Printed in the
United States
of America.

Dedicated
with loving appreciation
to Mr. and Mrs. Clifford Warren,
who gave me my wife

CONTENTS

LIFE is your most precious possession. Don't take it for granted.

Right now, you are either *wasting* your life, *spending* your life, or *investing* your life. It is *you* who determines which course to follow.

Jesus said, "The thief comes only to steal, and kill, and destroy; I came that they might have life, and might have it abundantly" (John 10:10).

"The thief . . ." Who is he? Ultimately, of course, he is Satan, the enemy of God and of good. But the thief always has assistance from people and circumstances. One man is robbed of life because of impatience: he always jumps the gun, only to find that the gun is aimed at him. Another person is robbed of abundant life because of selfish indulgence—food, sleep, sex, alcohol . . . you name it. Yes, there are many thieves that would like to keep us from enjoying Christ's abundant life: memories of past failures, fears of the future, a feeling that you're not important and that nobody cares. How tragic going through life and really not living!

But abundant life can be yours.

In his message about the Vine and the branches, Jesus Christ points out five spiritual secrets that lead to abundant life.

Please take these five spiritual secrets to heart: They work!

Warren W. Wiersbe
Moody Church, Chicago

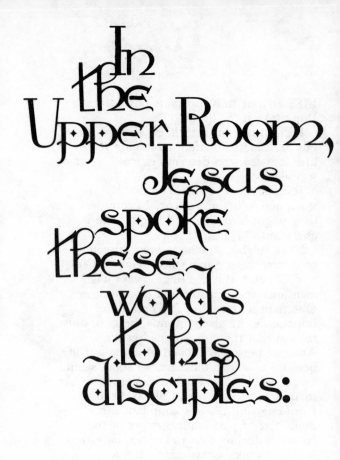

In the Upper Room, Jesus spoke these words to his disciples:

1 *I am the true vine, and My Father is the
   vinedresser.*

2 *Every branch in Me that does not bear
   fruit, He takes away; and every branch that
   bears fruit, He prunes it, that it may bear
   more fruit.*

3 *You are already clean because of the word
   which I have spoken to you.*

4 *Abide in Me, and I in you. As the branch
   cannot bear fruit of itself, unless it abides in
   the vine, so neither can you, unless you
   abide in Me.*

5 *I am the vine, you are the branches; he who
   abides in Me, and I in him, he bears much
   fruit; for apart from Me, you can do nothing.*

6 *If anyone does not abide in Me, he is
   thrown away as a branch, and dries up;
   and they gather them, and cast them into the
   fire, and they are burned.*

7 *If you abide in Me, and My words abide in
   you, ask whatever you wish, and it shall be
   done for you.*

8 *By this is My Father glorified, that you bear
   much fruit, and so prove to be My disciples.*

9 *Just as the Father has loved Me, I have also
   loved you; abide in My love.*

10 *If you keep My commandments, you will
   abide in My love; just as I have kept My
   Father's commandments, and abide in His
   love.*

11 *These things I have spoken to you, that My
   joy may be in you, and that your joy may
   be made full.*

12 This is My commandment, that you love one
another, just as I have loved you.
13 Greater love has no one than this, that one
lay down his life for his friends.
14 You are My friends, if you do what I
command you.
15 No longer do I call you slaves; for the slave
does not know what his master is doing; but
I have called you friends, for all things that
I have heard from My Father I have made
known to you.
16 You did not choose Me, but I chose you,
and appointed you, that you should go and
bear fruit, and that your fruit should
remain; that whatever you ask of the Father
in My name, He may give to you.
17 This I command you, that you love one
another.

(JOHN 15:1-17)

Secret One
The secret of living is fruitbearing.

Every branch in Me that does not bear fruit, He takes away; and every branch that bears fruit, He prunes it, that it may bear more fruit.

By this is My Father glorified, that you bear much fruit. . . .

You did not choose Me, but I chose you, and appointed you, that you should go and bear fruit, and that your fruit should remain. . . .

(JOHN 15:2, 8, 16)

"What and who am I?"
"Why am I here?"
You must answer these questions correctly if life is to have meaning for you. The man who calls a wrench a screwdriver, and who tries to use it as a screwdriver, is heading for frustration and failure. The person who does not know *who* and *what* he is will experience the same kind of frustration and failure. It is this identity crisis that has threatened and even destroyed many people in society today.

The Christian need not have an identity crisis. Jesus tells us who we are and why we are here. We are branches, and he is the Vine. We are here to bear fruit. Once you accept this simple fact, you are on the way to making your life meaningful and useful.

How did you become a branch in Christ, the Vine? By trusting him as your Savior and Lord. You have, by faith, a living relationship with Christ. You are not simply a member of a religious group; you are a living branch in the living Vine. When you yielded to Christ, a living union was formed between you and the Lord. Just as the branch gets its life from the vine, so the believer gets his life from Jesus Christ.

If you do not have this living union with

Christ, you cannot bear fruit. Fruit is the result of life. You can manufacture religious substitutes, but they will not be fruit.

The reason God saved you is that you might bear fruit in this world. You are living in a hungry world where people are starving for spiritual reality. *The branch does not bear fruit for the branch to eat, but for others to eat.* It is one of the great joys of life to share this fruit with others. That is why we are here.

Fruitbearing is a beautiful process. First there are the leaves; then the flowers; then the fruit. God provides the water from beneath and the sun from above. Day by day the branches develop; day by day the fruit is produced. If are looking for instant fruitfulness, you will be disappointed. Fruit must be cultivated. As we shall see later, the branch must abide in the Vine and draw upon his abundant life.

So, the reason God made you and saved you is that you might bear fruit in this world. You are a branch and he is the Vine. He has put you where you are that you might accomplish his special purpose. There is fruit to be produced where you are that nobody else can produce but you. *Accept the glory and the responsibility of being one of his branches.*

What is this fruit that God wants us to bear? It takes many different forms.

Winning others to Christ and helping them grow is fruit. Paul wrote to his friends at Rome, "Often I have planned to come to you . . . in order that I might obtain some fruit among you also, even as among the rest of the Gentiles" (Romans 1:13). There are many pictures in the Bible of the ministry of witnessing and leading others to Christ. "He who is wise wins souls," states Proverbs 11:30, and that word "wins" calls to mind a hunter taking his prey. Sometimes we must track down a lost soul in order to "take him" for Christ. Jesus compared evangelism to catching fish. "Follow Me, and I will make you become fishers of men" (Mark 1:17). Paul compared the evangelist to an ambassador (2 Corinthians 5:20), and Jesus said the soul-winner was a harvester (John 4:35). Zechariah 3:2 pictures the soul-winner as a fireman, snatching a burning brand out of the fire.

All of these pictures are true, because the ministry of leading others to Christ has many facets to it. It is wrong to focus on only one facet, because this will lead to a static, mechanical kind of a witness. There are times when soul-winning is a dangerous, dramatic experience as we snatch the brands out of the fire. At other times, we calmly and patiently sow the seed and ask God for a harvest. Sometimes others work with us and we cast the net into the sea and catch many fish. Again, sometimes we have that personal witness to one soul and as faithful ambassadors share the good news of the gospel.

But in all of these pictures, one factor is constant: *life.* The hunter, the fisherman, the harvester, the fireman, and the ambassador must have *life* if they are to get their work accomplished. This life can only come from Jesus Christ. As we are united to him and abide in him, his life flows in and through us, and we bear fruit. "I am the Vine, you are the branches." It is not *we* who do the work; it is he who does it in us and through us. We make ourselves available to him, and he makes his life available to us. Paul expressed it perfectly in 1 Corinthians 15:10—"But I labored even more than all of them, yet not I, but the grace of God with me."

It is a great joy and privilege to lead others to Christ. This ministry is not the automatic result of memorizing verses or passing courses. It is the result of allowing Christ's life to flow through you and bear fruit. "As the branch cannot bear fruit of itself, unless it abides in the vine, so neither can you, unless you abide in me" (John 15:4).

SECRET ONE
THE SECRET
OF LIVING
IS FRUITBEARING

Another kind of spiritual fruit is *practical holiness of life.* "But now being made free from sin, and become servants to God, ye have your fruit unto holiness, and the end everlasting life" (Romans 6:22, KJV). The theme of Romans 6 is victory over sin, and the fruit of this victory is a holy life. Never think of "holiness" as a brittle kind of piety such as the Pharisees practiced. Holiness is nothing else but the beauty and character of God displayed in our everyday lives. Holy living means more than victory over sin; it also means growth in character so that we become more like Jesus Christ. It has both negative and positive aspects: "Let us cleanse ourselves from all defilement of flesh and spirit, perfecting holiness in the fear of God" (2 Corinthians 7:1). As we share the life of Christ, we share the character of Christ.

Many people try to achieve holiness of life by means of some formula or religious discipline. Their system works for a time, and then they experience failure and frustration. Holiness is to the inner man what health is to the outer man; and both of them are a by-product of life. The person who eats properly, exercises, keeps clean, and gets the right amount of rest, will usually enjoy good health. The Christian who abides in Christ and shares his life will produce the fruit of holiness. *You cannot manufacture holiness.* The

Pharisees tried to do this and Jesus called them hypocrites. Holiness of life must come from within. It is fruit that we bear because we are branches in the Vine.

A third kind of fruit he enables us to bear is *the sharing of what we possess.* When Paul gathered a missionary offering from the Gentiles for the poor saints in Jerusalem, he called the offering "fruit." "When therefore I have performed this, and have sealed to them this fruit, I will come by you into Spain" (Romans 15:28, KJV). One of the characteristics of the early Christians was their joyful sharing of their possessions. It was not communism; it was Christian compassion. "And all that believed were together, and had all things common; and sold their possessions and goods, and parted them to all men, as every man had need" (Acts 2:44, 45, KJV). God has not commanded us to follow their exact example, but he has encouraged us to share what we have with others. "But whoever has the world's goods, and beholds his brother in need and closes his heart against him, how does the love of God abide in him?" (1 John 3:17).

Giving to God and, in his name, to others, is not something that we *do;* it is the result of what we *are.* When the branch is receiving life from the Vine, *it cannot help but give.* The branch exists to give! For the branch, *giving* and *living* are synonymous. To live is to give; to give is to live. The believer cannot selfishly hold on to whatever material blessings God gives him. If he is abiding in the Vine, he cannot help but give.

Christian character is a fourth kind of fruit, and it is described in Galatians 5:22, 23: "But the fruit of the Spirit is love, joy, peace, patience, kindness, goodness, faithfulness, gentleness, self-control . . ." Who does not want to have these qualities in his life! How different life becomes when you produce the fruit of the Spirit! The world has substitutes for these Christian graces, but it cannot duplicate them. Certainly unsaved people enjoy love, but not that deep *agape* love that comes from the heart of God. "We love, because He first loved us" (1 John 4:19). The world manufactures entertainment and even happiness, but it cannot manufacture that deep joy that comes from Christ. You can purchase *sleep,* but you cannot purchase *peace.* All of these marvelous qualities are spiritual fruit that only the Holy Spirit can produce when we, as branches, are drawing upon the life of the Vine.

Each of us wants to improve himself. There are weaknesses in our lives that we want to remove, and there are strengths that we want to develop. How do we do it? *By being branches in the Vine.* As the life of Christ comes in, we find old things passing

21

away and new things taking their place. Just as the face of nature takes on new beauty and power when the spring life comes in, so the Christian experiences new beauty when Christ's life comes in. Christian character—the fruit of the Spirit—cannot be manufactured in our own strength. Only the life of Christ within can produce this fruit.

"Bearing fruit in every good work" (Colossians 1:10); this is another kind of spiritual fruit that we bear as his branches. We are not saved by our good works; we are saved "by grace . . . through faith" (Ephesians 2:8, 9). But the result of salvation is always service. "Let your light so shine before men, that they may see your good works, and glorify your Father which is in heaven" (Matthew 5:16, KJV).

The unsaved person cannot perform any good works. He is dead as far as things spiritual are concerned, and he can only do "dead works" (Hebrews 9:14). But when the life of Christ moves in, the result is service for God, "being fruitful in every good work." And the beautiful thing about these good works is that *they are tailor-made for each individual believer.* We are "created in Christ Jesus for good works, which God prepared beforehand, that we should walk in them" (Ephesians 2:10). Each Christian has his own ministry to fulfill, and no

Christian is competing with any other
Christian in the will of God.

Some of the branches produce their
"good works" fruit in their own homes.
Others serve Christ in stores and offices,
or even in the cabs of trucks or the cabins
of jet planes. The teacher, the builder, the
doctor, the city official, the gardener, the
printer—all of these and many more serve
Jesus Christ (if they are Christians) by
accomplishing the good works he has
planned for them. In the Christian life,
there is no such division as "secular" and
"sacred." "Whether, then, you eat or drink
or whatever you do, do all to the glory of
God" (1 Corinthians 10:31). A Christian
pilot can serve and glorify the Lord just as
much as the missionaries he is flying to the
field.

This tremendous truth elevates your
vocation, whatever it is, and makes it a
ministry for the Lord. Of course, there are
some vocations that a believer would not
want to enter because in them he could
not glorify God. But God can use you in
any honorable calling to bring glory to his
name. You can be "fruitful in every good
work" and serve Jesus Christ.

Praising and thanking God is another kind
of fruit. "By him therefore let us offer the
sacrifice of praise to God continually, that
is, the fruit of our lips giving thanks to his

name" (Hebrews 13:15, KJV). The Old
Testament worshiper brought the fruit of
his field for a sacrifice to God. The New
Testament worshiper brings the fruit of his
lips. *By our words, we praise and glorify God.*

Some Christians find it difficult and
embarrassing to witness and praise the
Lord before others, especially unbelievers.
In our own strength, we can never do this;
but as branches in the Vine, we can receive
his life and bear "the fruit of the lips."
Praising God then becomes a natural thing,
not a forced thing, and we do it joyfully
and not with a feeling of guilt. A
manufactured witness is a dead witness.
Praise that is forced is empty praise. But
when our words are the fruit of our union
with Christ, they are alive and exciting.
Our witness has power to it. We do not
need to be afraid or ashamed when it
comes to sharing Christ with others. God
will produce the "fruit of the lips" and
others will be able to eat it.

These, then, are some of the different
kinds of fruit God wants us to bear in our
lives: witnessing and winning souls,
holiness of life, character, sharing, good
works, and praise and testimony. But our
Lord also makes it clear that this
fruitbearing is to be a continuous

experience: "fruit . . . more fruit . . . much fruit." He said, "By this is My Father glorified, that you bear much fruit, and so prove to be My disciples" (John 15:8).

How is this increase possible? There are two answers to the question.

First, as you and I as branches continue to abide in Christ, we establish a deeper relationship with him. The hindrances that affect the fruitbearing are removed, and he is able to do more in us and through us. The longer we abide in Christ, the better fitted we become to bear more fruit.

Second, the fruit that we bear *has seed in it for more fruit!* As others partake of this fruit, they also begin to bear fruit; and this results in "more fruit . . . much fruit . . ." This points up the difference between "results" and "fruit." It is possible to "get results" in our Christian service, and even have impressive statistics; but none of these "results" will bear fruit. It is only as we bear fruit that the seed is there for more fruit.

The following story has been told of both D. L. Moody and Sam Jones, the Methodist evangelist. No matter; the lesson is clear. The evangelist met a drunk on the street, and the drunk said, "Say, I'm one of your converts!" The evangelist replied, "You must be one of *my* converts—you certainly aren't one of the Lord's converts." A good illustration of the difference between "fruit" and "results." Where there is true fruit, there is life; and where there is life, there is the seed for more fruit.

🐛 The secret of living is fruitbearing. God did not create you, and Christ did not die for you that you might go through life *getting*. God created you and Christ purchased you that you might invest your life *giving*. If you refuse to bear fruit, you will miss the true meaning and glory of the Christian life. If you yield to Christ and permit his life to create his fruit through you, then you will really live.

Are you willing to be a branch? Tell him that you are.

Are you willing for his life to work in and through you? Then, tell him.

By an act of faith, yield yourself to Christ for the purpose of bearing fruit, for the purpose of fulfilling that wonderful plan God has for you and you alone.

Secret One
The Secret
of living
is fruitbearing.

Secret Two
The secret
of fruitbearing
is abiding.

*Abide in me, and I in
you. As the branch
cannot bear fruit of
itself, unless it abides in
the vine, so neither can
you, unless you abide in
Me.*

*If you abide in Me,
and My words abide in
you, ask whatever you
wish, and it shall be done
for you.*
(JOHN 15:4, 7)

At least twelve times in John 15, Jesus uses the word *abide*. Why? Because abiding is the secret of fruitbearing. The branch does not bear fruit by struggling, but by abiding. If you were to walk through a vineyard, you would not detect tension and struggle among the branches. Instead, you would discover a calm, confident *resting*—an *abiding*—as the branches draw their life from the Vine.

In the Christian life, there is a difference between *union* and *communion.* When you trusted Christ to save you, the Holy Spirit united you to him in a living relationship. You became a branch in the Vine; a living union was formed. But this once-for-all union is the basis for communion—maintaining a moment-by-moment fellowship with the Lord so that his life is shared with you. The branch that tries to go it alone will never bear fruit.

We must be careful to distinguish between his supernatural life and our own natural qualities. There are many people who by nature are quiet and unassuming, but this attitude is not necessarily Christian humility. Others are naturally optimistic and effervescent, but this may not be Christian joy. How can you tell the difference? In two ways. First, when our abiding in Christ produces true spiritual fruit, *it is beyond anything that we can do and we know it.* Second, because this is true, when there is spiritual fruit, *God gets the glory.* People recognize that it is God at work in our lives doing in and through us what we could never do for ourselves. Certainly the Holy Spirit can use personality traits, such as Peter's courage or Paul's self-control; but usually he has to help us *overcome* these traits when we depend upon them and not on the Lord. Peter's courage almost made him a murderer when he struck at Malchus with his sword.

How do we abide in Christ? Historically, two schools of thought have developed around the answer to that important question: the "quietists" and the "activists." The first group says, "You do nothing. You simply yield to him and let him have his way. Christ lives in you and he wants to use you the way the hand uses the glove. All the glove has to do is surrender." But the second group replies, "Not on your life! We are not dead gloves but living people. God never violates our personality and forces himself on us. We must yield, but we must obey as well. We must actively read the Bible, pray, worship, and do all that he wants us to do."

Actually, both answers contain a measure
of truth. Surrender is important, and
cooperation is also important. Abiding is
not a passive thing, like a glove on a hand,
because a glove does not have intellect,
emotions, and will the way a person does.
The glove can do nothing else but
surrender! On the other hand, abiding is
not such an active thing that we must
manufacture the experience. Everybody
has a "spiritual formula" for you to follow:
A + B + C = D. But formulas for the
spiritual life are not always as neat and
surefire as chemical formulas or cake
recipes.

Paul gives us the best answer in
Philippians 2:12, 13—". . . work out your
salvation with fear and trembling; for it is
God who is at work in you, both to will
and to work for his good pleasure." God
works in, we work out. As we surrender,
God works in; as we obey, God works out.
Abiding involves keeping in fellowship
with the Vine so that God can work in us.

Certainly abiding involves spending time
with the Lord in meditation and prayer.
"If you abide in Me, and My words abide
in you . . ." (John 15:7). "If you keep my
commandments, you will abide in My
love . . ." (John 15:10). You cannot *keep* his
commandments if you do not *know* them,
and you cannot know them personally
apart from his Word. "But his delight is in

the law of the Lord, and in His law he meditates day and night" (Psalm 1:2).

Prayer is also a part of abiding. "If you abide in Me, and My words abide in you, ask whatever you wish, and it shall be done for you" (John 15:7). The better we know the Word of God, the better we can pray; for the Word of God reveals the will of God. "And this is the confidence which we have before Him, that if we ask anything according to His will, He hears us" (1 John 5:14). Of course, prayer is much more than asking. It also involves giving thanks, expressing love and worship, and also confessing sin.

Confession is a third factor in abiding. Sin always breaks our communion with God. "If we say that we have fellowship with Him and yet walk in the darkness, we lie and do not practice the truth" (1 John 1:6). It is important that we keep our hearts and minds clean and that we confess all known sin. David even asked to be cleansed from "hidden faults" (Psalm 19:12)! There are sins that we commit that even we may not know about.

A fourth factor is a desire to do his will. "If you keep My commandments, you will abide in My love" (John 15:10). "I delight to do Thy will, O my God; Thy Law is within my heart" (Psalm 40:8). God's will for our lives is that we bear fruit and glorify him. His plan will be worked out in

different ways with different people, and
we must be willing for God to have his
way. "Nevertheless not what I will, but
what thou wilt" (Mark 14:36).

It is the Holy Spirit who encourages and
enables us to abide. He teaches us the
Word; he enables us to pray; he reveals
our sins; he gives us the inward desire to
obey God. The Spirit of God uses the
Word of God and prayer to strengthen
our communion with Christ. This
experience of abiding is not always
accompanied by "spiritual feelings" or
unusual emotional changes. Then how can
we know when we are truly abiding in
Christ?

We never have to ask "Am I abiding in
Christ?" because there will be several
evidences in our lives when we are in
communion with the Lord.

The first evidence, and the most
obvious, is *fruit.* "He who abides in Me,
and I in him, he bears much fruit; for
apart from Me, you can do nothing" (John
15:5). If we are maintaining a close
fellowship with him, then the result will be
fruit in and through our lives. We will not
need to manufacture "results" in our own
strength. The Holy Spirit will produce
fruit, and this fruit will remain.

33

This means that God will use *us* to touch the lives of others and help win them to Christ. It may not be our privilege to actually lead them to the Savior, but we will be a part of that miracle experience. My own conversion was the fruit of many different branches—a praying pastor, praying friends, faithful Sunday school teachers, a dedicated evangelist, to name but a few—and when I did trust the Lord, I was standing *alone* in the back of a high school auditorium listening to a man preach! For many years, that evangelist did not know that he had produced fruit in my life that night. In fact, he told me later that he had gone home from the meeting disappointed. God had given some fruit but he did not know it. You may have to wait until you see the Lord in glory before you will know what fruit has been produced in your life.

If you are growing in holy living, and experiencing victory over temptation, then you are abiding in Christ. The *absence* of temptation is not a proof of abiding; the *presence* of temptation and testing is the proof. Bearing "fruit unto holiness" (Romans 6:22, KJV) is a daily process, not a finished matter. As we grow in Christ, we conquer new areas in our lives; and the beautiful "fruit of the Spirit" is more and more evident. If you find yourself growing in "love, joy, peace, patience, kindness, goodness, faithfulness, gentleness, self-control," then you know you are abiding in Christ.

You will also find yourself developing new values and wanting to invest what you have for God's glory. Sharing what we have with others is "fruit" (Romans 15:28). Christians are not only forgiven, but they are also forgiving and *for giving.* "It is more blessed to give than to receive" (Acts 20:35, KJV) is their philosophy of life. The Christian who is not abiding in Christ is selfish; he misses the joy of bearing and sharing.

As you abide in Christ, you will find many ways to work for him. You will not have to be threatened or bribed: working for Christ will be the natural result of walking with Christ and abiding in him. You will discover and develop your gifts and go to work in his church as he leads you.

You will find yourself praising the Lord as you abide in him. You will praise him for his blessings, and you will praise him for the burdens of life as well. You will praise him when the way is bright and clear, and you will praise him when the way is dark and perplexing. The Christian who does not abide in Christ gives thanks *occasionally* for *some* things; but the abiding Christian gives thanks *always* for *all* things. Through Christ you will "continually offer

up a sacrifice of praise to God . . . "
(Hebrews 13:15).

If we do not abide, we do not bear fruit;
and if we do not bear fruit, the Father,
who is the Vinedresser, must deal with us.
"If anyone does not abide in Me, he is
thrown away as a branch, and dries up;
and they gather them, and cast them into
the fire, and they are burned" (John 15:6).
Some apply this warning to "professed"
Christians, people who are not truly saved
and therefore cannot bear fruit. But how
would a "professed" Christian become a
branch of the vine? When Jesus said "You
are the branches" (John 15:5), he was
speaking to saved people who had been
cleansed through faith in him (John 15:3).
Judas, the counterfeit believer, had already
gone out (John 13:21-30).

Is Jesus telling us that, if we do not bear
fruit, we lose our salvation? I think not,
and for several reasons. To begin with, the
emphasis in this message about the vine
and the branches is on *service,* not *salvation.*
Jesus is not telling us how to get saved, or
even how to get others saved, but how to
live for him now that we are saved. The
emphasis is on communion, not union; it is
on fellowship and discipleship, not sonship.
He is addressing us as servants who are his
friends (John 15:15), and he is instructing
us how to serve him.

It is God the Father who "takes away"

the branch that does not bear fruit (John 15:1, 2). It is not God the Son who does it. God the Father has appointed his Son to be the judge. "For not even the Father judges anyone, but He has given all judgment to the Son" (John 5:22). If the consigning of a fruitless branch to the fire meant a soul being sent to eternal judgment, then it would be done by the Son, not the Father.

What is the Father's relationship to the branch? He is the Vinedresser. He seeks to make the branch more fruitful, even to the extent of pruning the branch and cutting away excess wood and leaves (John 15:2). If the branch refuses to abide and bear fruit, then the Father can remove it to make way for a fruitful branch. This is known as spiritual discipline, or chastening. If the branch does not respond to the Father's ministry, then the Father may have to take it away. Paul expressed the same thought in a different context—athletics. "And everyone who competes in the games exercises self-control in all things. . . . but I buffet my body and make it my slave, lest possibly, after I have preached to others, I myself should be disqualified" (1 Corinthians 9:25, 27). Is Paul suggesting that he was afraid he might go to hell? I think not. He was telling us of his fear of *losing his ministry and losing his reward.*

No matter how little fruit you may be producing, it is evidence that you are abiding in Christ. The Father sees that fruit and rejoices in it. He then does all he can to help you produce "more fruit . . . . much fruit" (John 15:2, 5). The last thing the Father wants to do is take away your opportunity for glorifying him in fruitbearing. But a fruitless branch is a disgrace to the Vinedresser! Certainly the fruitless believer ought to confess his sins and have his fellowship restored; then he can bear fruit for God's glory.

A second evidence that you are abiding in Christ is *the Father's pruning.* "Every branch that bears fruit, He prunes it, that it may bear more fruit" (John 15:2). What is this pruning process? It is the Father cutting out of our lives the things that hinder us from being more fruitful. God always wants us to reach our greatest potential. This explains why abiding Christians are often suffering Christians. They experience the Father's pruning, and it hurts.

What does the Father cut away from our lives? Anything that keeps the life of the Vine from producing more fruit, much fruit. If the life goes to leaf, he cuts away the excess leaves. Of themselves, leaves are

not bad; but if they rob us of fruit, they
are sinful. The abiding Christian is not
constantly dealing with "bad things"; he is
often dealing with "good things." God told
Abraham to leave his home and family,
but Abraham took his father along. The
father had to die before God could
continue his work in Abraham's life. But
Abraham took his nephew Lot with him,
and Lot also had to be cut away. Then it
was his son Ishmael, whom he fathered
through Hagar. And then it was his
beloved son Isaac who was given to him by
the Lord. (Though God gave him back.)
Expect to be pruned if you abide in Christ.

Have you ever wondered why some
believers seem to "sail through life" in
constant sunshine, while others experience
suffering and loss? To be sure, God has
different plans for each of his children;
but this much is true: *believers who abide in
Christ can expect to suffer.* The Father's knife
is ready to cut away anything in their lives
that is keeping them from bearing more
fruit for his glory. The Father may *hurt*
you, but he will never *harm* you. His
pruning is for your good and his glory,
and that is all that really counts.

When you first start abiding in Christ,
you find the sinful things of your life
falling away as his life takes control. It is a
thrilling thing to live in victory over the
gross things of the flesh and the appetites

39

of the world. But as your experience deepens, you start to experience the pruning process; and God starts to cut away things that you think are good. "Why, Lord?" is the prayer often on your lips. And his answer is clear: "I want you to bear more fruit. The secret of living is fruitbearing, and the more fruit you bear, *the more you will live.*" The abiding Christian does not choose between the good and the bad; an unsaved person can do that. The abiding Christian chooses between the better and the best. He is not discouraged when the Father prunes his life and cuts away something that he considers dear, because he knows he will receive something far more precious in return.

Expect to be pruned if you are abiding in Christ. This is the only way to bear more fruit and glorify the Father.

 There is a third evidence of abiding; it is *a growing sense of weakness.* "I am the vine, you are the branches" (John 15:5). The Father often has to remind us that we are *branches* and not the Vine itself. He permits us to go through circumstances that bring out our weakness and his strength. He repeatedly teaches us, "Without me, you can do nothing."

This is one reason for the testings that we experience in life. Have you ever noticed that God often tests his children in their strongest points? Satan tempts us in our weakest points to bring out the worst in us, but God tests us in our strongest points to bring out the best in us. If we fail in our *strong* points, think of how much greater we would fail in our weak points!

Abraham's strongest point was his faith, and that is exactly where the Lord tested him. God permitted a famine to come to the land, and Abraham went down to Egypt to save himself. He failed the test. Moses' strongest point was his meekness; yet he lost his temper one day and failed to glorify God. Peter's greatest strength was his courage; yet he became a coward when confronted by a little maid who asked him about Jesus. Peter had boasted that he would even die with the Lord Jesus! He found out how weak he was and that, apart from Christ, he could do nothing.

After you have been abiding in Christ for a long time, you may be tempted to feel stronger than you really are. You may feel capable of handling life in your own wisdom and power. Beware! You are heading for certain failure and shame. Jesus said, "Apart from Me, you can do nothing" (John 15:5). *Nothing.* Of yourself, you are a weak branch, good for nothing but the fire. But in Christ you have all the strength you need to bear fruit and glorify God. *Your weakness is your strength.* God will see to it that you are reminded of your weakness, even if he has to bring you very low to do it. "Most gladly, therefore, I will rather boast about my weaknesses, that the power of Christ may dwell in me" (2 Corinthians 12:9).

If you are abiding in Christ, you will know it because *he will answer your prayers.* "If you abide in Me, and My words abide in you, ask whatever you wish, and it shall be done for you" (John 15:7).

Prayer is not only a *cause* but also a *result* of abiding. As we pray, we abide; as we abide, we pray more, and more deeply. Prayer is not a "religious exercise" that we perform out of obedience, as good as that might be. Prayer is the very breath and heartbeat of our lives. Prayer is part of a beautiful relationship between us and God: he speaks to us in his Word, and we speak to him from our hearts. Prayer is not simply a servant showing up for orders from his master. Prayer is a friend sharing his heart with his Friend and growing in love and faith. Jesus does not call us slaves; he calls us friends. Because he is our Friend, we want to talk with him and listen to him talk with us.

You dare not separate prayer from the Word of God. "If you abide in Me, and My words abide in you . . ." (John 15:7). As we read the Word of God, we discover God's will, what he wants to give us. As we further meditate on his Word, our hearts are gradually changed, and we start to desire what he desires. "Delight yourself in the Lord; and He will give you the desires of your heart" (Psalm 37:4). Apart from the inner working of the Word in our hearts, we would never desire what he wants us to desire. Our desires would be selfish and sinful, and our prayers would be selfish and sinful. "You ask and do not receive, because you ask with wrong motives, so that you may spend it on your pleasures" (James 4:3).

Your Father wants to answer prayer. If you are abiding in Christ, and if his Word abides in you, then you will pray in his will and he will answer. "And this is the confidence which we have before Him, that if we ask anything according to His will, He hears us" (1 John 5:14). It has well been said that prayer is not getting man's will done in heaven, but getting God's will done on earth. It is not overcoming God's reluctance but laying hold of God's willingness.

If you find your prayers becoming

selfish, or if you find prayer becoming a deadening experience, a burden instead of a joy, then it may be you are not abiding in Christ. If you pray but God does not answer, something may have happened to your communion with him. "If I regard wickedness in my heart, the Lord will not hear" (Psalm 66:18). Prayer is both a thermometer and a thermostat in the Christian life. It helps to regulate our "spiritual temperature," but it also registers the devotion of our hearts.

What a joy it is to have God answer prayer! What confidence it gives you to know that you can take "everything to God in prayer" and he will hear and answer! He does not always give us what we ask, but he does give us what we need, *when we need it*. This is one of the evidences of abiding.

A fifth evidence of abiding is *love for Christ and his people*. "Just as the Father has loved Me, I have also loved you; abide in My love. . . . This is My commandment, that you love one another, just as I have loved you" (John 15:9, 12). God is love, and if we are sharing his life, we must experience his love. And if we experience that love, we must *express* that love to others.

There is a danger that our abiding life may become self-centered and isolated. We get so wrapped up in a relationship with God that we neglect or ignore the people around us. But this kind of "abiding" is false. The closer we grow to the Lord, the more of his love we will want to share with others. *Christian love is simply treating others the way God has treated us.* Jesus commanded us to "love one another, just as I have loved you" (John 15:12). "Beloved, if God so loved us, we also ought to love one another. . . . We love, because He first loved us" (1 John 4:11, 19).

You first experience this love when you trust Christ for salvation: "the love of God has been poured out within our hearts through the Holy Spirit who was given to us" (Romans 5:5). As you abide in Christ, the "fruit of the Spirit" begins to appear, and the first is love. This Christian love is not a sentimental feeling that comes and goes; no, it is a deep experience through the Spirit that does not fluctuate with changing feelings or circumstances. This love enables us to see Christ in others in spite of their faults and mistakes (1 Peter 4:8: "Above all, keep fervent in your love for one another, because love covers a multitude of sins"). There may be people we do not like because of their personalities, or with whom we disagree; but we will love them in Christ.

The test of this love is sacrifice. "Greater love has no one than this, that one lay down his life for his friends" (John 15:13). The kind of love our Lord is talking about—*agape* love—is love that gives, that sacrifices, that willingly pays the price that others might be helped. It should be no problem for us to lay down our lives for our friends when Christ laid down his life *for his enemies!*

This *agape* love shines out against the dark background of the world's hatred for Christ and the Christian. "If the world hates you, you know that it has hated Me before it hated you. If you were of the world, the world would love its own; but because you are not of the world, but I chose you out of the world, therefore the world hates you" (John 15:18, 19). By "the world," of course, Jesus means *society apart from God,* that system of values, philosophies, ideas, goals, and experiences that is wholly separated from God and is even anti-God. He is not speaking about the world of nature or the world of people, although the "world system" can and does use people and things to promote its cause. The more you abide in Christ, the less you love the world system and the more you love Christ and his people. Conversely, the less you abide in Christ, the more the world will love you,

and the less comfortable you will feel with
the people of God.

Christians are the light of the world and
the salt of the earth (Matthew 5:13-16).
Our light shows up the world's darkness;
our purity shows up the world's sin. The
more we abide in Christ, the brighter the
light shines and the purer our lives
become, *and the more the world hates us.*
"And indeed, all who desire to live godly
in Christ Jesus will be persecuted"
(2 Timothy 3:12). Were it not for the love
of God's people within the fellowship of
the church, we would find it difficult to
face the hatred of the world. It is sad
when Christians fail to love one another,
for that failure makes the church just like
the world. If we find ourselves lacking in
love for the brethren, it may be a sign we
are not abiding in Christ as we should.

When the believer is abiding in Christ,
he experiences *an inner joy.* "These things I
have spoken to you, that My joy may be in
you, and that your joy may be made full"
(John 15:11). Christian joy is not the
absence of trial or trouble; it is a deep
peace and confidence in the midst of trial
and trouble. The very hour in which Jesus
spoke those words was one of tremendous

pressure and challenge for him. Judas
would betray him; Peter would deny him;
his own followers would forsake him and
flee. He would be arrested, falsely accused,
humiliated, beaten, and then crucified. He
would even be forsaken by his Father! *Yet
Jesus was able to give his joy to his disciples!* It
was a joy in the midst of sorrow, a
confidence in the midst of man's failure
and sin.

The world offers entertainment, and
even a bit of happiness; but only Christ
can give joy; and this joy comes from our
abiding in him. "In Thy presence is
fulness of joy" (Psalm 16:11). "For the
kingdom of God is not eating and
drinking, but righteousness and peace and
joy in the Holy Spirit" (Romans 14:17).
This joy comes from Christ, not from
ourselves or the circumstances around us.
"And my soul shall rejoice in the Lord; it
shall exult in His salvation" (Psalm 35:9).

One of the first symptoms of
backsliding—not abiding in Christ—is a
loss of joy. When David sinned and tried
to hide it from God, he ceased to sing and
praise the Lord. "When I kept silent about
my sin, my body wasted away through my
groaning all day long" (Psalm 32:3). When
David finally confessed his sin, he prayed,
"Restore to me the joy of Thy salvation"
(Psalm 51:12). Spiritual joy is the result of
abiding in Christ; loss of that joy is an

evidence that we are not abiding in Christ.
The only way to restore that communion,
and the resulting joy, is through
confession. "If we confess our sins, He is
faithful and righteous to forgive us our
sins and to cleanse us from all
unrighteousness" (1 John 1:9).

Here, then, are some of the evidences
that we are abiding in Christ: We bear
fruit for God's glory. We experience the
Father's pruning that we might bear more
fruit. We have a sense of weakness and
know that we are only the branches; Christ
is the Vine. We have our prayers
answered. We love the brethren and are
hated by the world. We experience a deep
joy in spite of circumstances.

To be sure, not every abiding believer
will have all of these blessings in the same
degree at the same time. But they will be
present in some measure, and they will be
strong enough to be evident. Others may
see these blessings in us better than we do!

It is good for us as branches to examine
ourselves regularly to see if we are abiding
in Christ. We want to bear fruit, and the
secret of fruitbearing is abiding.

Secret One
The secret
of living
is fruitbearing.

Secret Two
The secret
of fruitbearing
is abiding.

Secret Three
The secret
of abiding
is obeying.

If you keep My commandments, you will abide in My love; just as I have kept My Father's commandments, and abide in His love. . . . You are My friends, if you do what I command you.
(JOHN 15:10, 14)

It is a fundamental law of the universe, ordained of God, that obedience leads to abiding. The person who obeys the laws of health will abide in health. The farmer who obeys the laws of nature will abide and enjoy the fruits of his labor. The scientist who obeys the laws of science will abide and be able to accomplish things. God has written certain laws and principles into this world, and we cannot disobey them without suffering.

I live not far from the world's busiest airport, O'Hare in Chicago. Often I see huge planes taking off and landing, and I never cease to marvel at the fact that those gigantic machines can ever get off the ground and stay in the air. The law of gravity dictates that it cannot be done. But by obeying other laws, the aeronautical engineers can make the planes fly. If the pilot stops obeying, he stops abiding!

One reason we are facing ecological problems and crises is because we did not obey God's laws. Had we obeyed, we would still be abiding in a world with plenty of pure air and water and a growing supply of natural resources. But we did not obey, so we cannot abide. *The secret of abiding is obeying.*

Why is this so? Why did God make obedience the secret of abiding?

To begin with, *God obeys his own laws.*

There are times when he performs miracles and brings a higher law into play, but God's usual mode of working is to obey his own laws that he has built into the universe. Because he does obey these laws, we have the changes of seasons, we have harvests, and we can harness the tremendous power that the universe holds. All of science is based on the fact that God obeys his own laws. From the splitting of the atom to the charting of a distant planet, man can depend on God's laws. If God once disobeyed his own laws, the universe would fall apart.

The source of evil in this world is man, not God. It was because of the first man's disobedience to God's law that sin came into the world. It is because men and women continue to disobey God's will that evil grows and destroys in this world. The same divine law that gives the farmer corn when he plants corn also gives the sinner sorrow and death when he sins, for we reap what we sow. "Do not be deceived, God is not mocked; for whatever a man sows, this will he also reap. For the one who sows to his own flesh shall from the flesh reap corruption, but the one who sows to the Spirit shall from the Spirit reap eternal life" (Galatians 6:7, 8).

Since God obeys his own laws, and the universe abides in him because he does, then when we obey his Word, we too will

abide in him. To disobey God is to fly in
the face of the whole universe! This
explains why the disobedient person has so
much trouble, not only inwardly, but also
outwardly. When the child of God obeys
the will of God, everything in the world
works for him; but when the child of God
disobeys the will of God, everything works
against him. There are times when
obedience seems to bring difficulty; but the
trial is only temporary, and the result will
be blessing. Paul and Silas obeyed God in
going to Philippi, and ended up in prison.
But the result was great blessing in the
salvation of the jailer and his family, and
the establishing of a new church.

Everything in the universe obeys God
except man, and man has the most to gain
by obeying and the most to lose by
disobeying! The biggest stars and the
tiniest cells all obey God's will. This is what
keeps the universe together. "Fire and hail,
snow and clouds; stormy wind, fulfilling
His word" (Psalm 148:8). No part of
natural creation would ever think of
questioning God's will, let alone disobeying
it. Only man questions and disobeys God's
will, because man (by God's grace) has a
will of his own. He was created to make
decisions, and he can decide to disobey
God.

This is the second reason why obedience
is the secret of abiding: *obedience involves*

the will. We do not abide simply by having thoughts about God's will or even feelings about God's will. We abide when we obey God's will, and this means submitting our will. Of course, we ought to do the will of God from the heart, and we ought to be intelligent about it; but the important thing is *doing it.* No amount of thoughts in the mind and feelings in the heart can compensate for disobedience of the will.

Too many Christians settle for an intellectual experience. They study the Bible, learn facts and definitions, and try to explain doctrines; but they never obey what God tells them. Other believers have only an *emotional* experience: they try to generate and cultivate "spiritual feelings" that help them "enjoy the Lord." While sincere emotion is certainly a part of the Christian life, it is not the only part.

We must realize that *the will* is the center of the Christian life. We obey God, not because we feel like it, but because it is the right thing to do. And we should graduate from obeying *because we have to* into obeying *because we want to.* Jonah finally obeyed God; but deep within, he still wanted his own way. "Doing the will of God from the heart" (Ephesians 6:6) is the best description of the kind of obedience God is seeking.

Our Lord uses himself as the example of obedience. "If you keep My commandments, you will abide in My love; just as I have kept My Father's commandments, and abide in His love" (John 15:10). "My food is to do the will of Him who sent me, and to accomplish His work" (John 4:34). "I do not seek My own will, but the will of Him who sent Me" (John 5:30). "For I have come down from heaven, not to do My own will, but the will of Him who sent Me" (John 6:38). "I delight to do Thy will, O my God: thy law is within my heart" (Psalm 40:8).

Because the Son loved the Father, he obeyed his will, no matter what the cost. Jesus did not permit people to turn him from the will of God. When Peter suggested that Jesus not go to the cross, Jesus replied, "Get behind Me, Satan! You are a stumbling-block to Me; for you are not setting your mind on God's interests, but man's" (Matthew 16:23). Our Lord's obedience to the will of God cost him his life. "He humbled Himself by becoming obedient to the point of death, even death on a cross" (Philippians 2:8). This is what he meant by "taking up a cross." He meant obedience in spite of suffering, shame, and sacrifice.

You and I will do everything possible to avoid obedience. And yet obedience is the very key to God's blessing. King Saul tried to substitute sacrifice for obedience, but God would not accept the substitute (1 Samuel 15:22). Jesus told a story about two sons who were given orders by their father, and one of the boys substituted words for obedience (Matthew 21:28-32). His words were not accepted. In his parable of the talents (Matthew 25:14-30), Jesus told about a one-talent man who tried to substitute excuses for obedience; and he was judged. *There is no substitute for obedience.*

As God's children, we should want to obey him so that we might abide in him. The blessings we receive come from the abiding, just as the abiding comes from the obeying. These blessings are not a reward for obeying; they are a result of abiding. We must never bargain with God. We must never say, "Lord, I will obey what you command if you will do for me what I want done." Our obedience must be complete and unconditional. "What shall I do, Lord?" (Acts 22:10).

The tragic results of disobedience are recorded in the Bible, beginning with man's first rebellion in Genesis 3. Adam and Eve did not abide because they did not obey. In spite of occasional failures, Abraham obeyed God and maintained his fellowship with him. Abraham became "the friend of God" (James 2:23), while Lot became a friend of the world. The nation of Israel disobeyed God and did not abide in their land. First they were carried to Babylon; then they were scattered throughout the world. "See, I am setting before you today a blessing and a curse: the blessing, if you listen to the commandments of the Lord your God, which I am commanding you today; and the curse, if you do not listen to the commandments of the Lord your God . . ." (Deuteronomy 11:26-28).

Obedience releases power. When the scientist obeys the laws of science, built into nature by God, then he can release power. The farmer who obeys the laws of growth will release power and produce fruit. But when we disobey these laws, the power that is released will destroy us and not help us. Disobey the laws that govern electricity and you may kill yourself and others. Obey them, and you will abide.

But obeying is one of the most difficult things in the world! There is something perverse and selfish in our very nature that tells us, "Do it your own way! Don't bow down to anybody else!" We inherited this stubbornness from our first parents, and they got it by listening to Satan's, "Indeed, has God said. . . ?" (Genesis 3:1). Paul described our sad plight: "For I know that nothing good dwells in me, that is, in my flesh; for the wishing is present in me, but the doing of the good is not. For the good that I wish, I do not do; but I practice the very evil that I do not wish" (Romans 7:18, 19).

How can you and I obey God?

That is our next secret.

Secret One
The secret
of living
is fruitbearing.

Secret Two
The secret
of fruitbearing
is abiding.

Secret Three
The secret
of abiding
is obeying.

Secret Four
The secret
of obeying
is loving.

*Just as the Father has
loved Me, I have also
loved you; abide in My
love. If you keep My
commandments, you will
abide in My love; just as
I have kept My Father's
commandments, and
abide in His love."*
(JOHN 15:9, 10)
*If anyone loves Me, he
will keep My word. . . .
He who does not love Me
does not keep My Words....*
(JOHN 14:23, 24)
*If you love Me, you will
keep My commandments.*
(JOHN 14:15)

There are three levels of obedience.

We can obey God because *we have to;* this is the level of fear. There is, of course, a proper fear of God that is holy and good. It is not the fear that a slave shows to a master, but the respect that a son shows to a father. "Furthermore, we had earthly fathers to discipline us, and we respected them; shall we not much rather be subject to the Father of spirits, and live?" (Hebrews 12:9). If we willfully disobey God, he will chasten us. For this reason, we fear him.

But fear is not the best motive for obedience. "No longer do I call you slaves," said Jesus to his disciples (John 15:15), indicating that their relationship was much deeper. Fear can rob us of the real joys that God wants us to experience because we obey him. Because we are his children, we want to get closer to him; and fear builds walls instead of bridges.

The next level of obedience is selfishness: we obey because *we need to,* because we get something out of it! Peter illustrates this level when he asked Jesus, "Behold, we have left everything and followed You; what then will there be for us?" (Matthew 19:27). Children obey their parents because children are afraid of spankings. Teen-agers obey because they have learned that obedience can purchase favors! The young man who mows the lawn and cleans his room is going to have a better chance to get the keys to the car. And the girl who has helped mother in the kitchen is going to have a better chance to go shopping for new clothes. Selfish? Yes—but it works!

Many Christians live on this "bargain basement" level. Their obedience is measured by what God gives them; and if they do not get what they want, they often turn against God. They do not have the kind of obedience shown by the three Hebrews when Nebuchadnezzar threatened to throw them into the blazing furnace. "If it be so, our God whom we serve is able to deliver us from the furnace of blazing fire; and He will deliver us out of your hand, O king. But even if He does not, let it be known to you, O king, that we are not going to serve your gods or worship the golden image that you have set up" (Daniel 3:17, 18).

The highest motive for obedience is *love*. "If you love Me, you will keep My commandments" (John 14:15).

Why is love the highest motive for obedience?

For one thing, love centers on the giver,

not the gift. Love establishes a personal relationship with God no matter what he gives or what he withholds. Satan was sure that Job would curse God when Job lost his possessions and his health. If Job had been like some believers today, that is exactly what he would have done. Instead, he testified, "Though He slay me, I will hope in Him . . ." (Job 13:15). Where there is love, there can be no bargaining. Jacob, the great schemer and bargainer, forgot about the contract when he fell in love with Rachel! He willingly worked fourteen years to make her his own; "and they seemed to him but a few days because of his love for her" (Genesis 29:20).

Another reason is this: love does not measure sacrifice. "Greater love has no one than this, that one lay down his life for his friends" (John 15:13). Our Lord proved his love for us by going to the cross for us. He did not measure his sacrifice and give the least possible amount. He gave his all. If we love God, we do not measure the cost of obeying his Word. We simply obey. Like the father that rushes into the burning house to save his child, or the mother that plunges into the raging waters, we do not count the cost, but instead obey the loving impulses of the heart. Love that calculates is not true love.

Love is the highest motive for obedience because "God is love" (1 John 4:8). He gives his commandments because he loves us; and because we love him, we obey his commandments. We do not question them or seek to change them. We do not fear his will. "There is no fear in love; but perfect love casts out fear . . ." (1 John 4:18). As we obey, we experience the love of God in our hearts in a deep and satisfying way. "God is love, and the one who abides in love abides in God, and God abides in him" (1 John 4:16). "He who has My commandments and keeps them, he it is who loves Me; and he who loves Me shall be loved by My Father, and I will love him, and will disclose Myself to him" (John 14:21).

Love is the fulfillment of the law. If two people love each other, they do not need rules and regulations to govern their relationship. When a husband and wife love each other, they always try to do the things that please each other and help each other. There are laws that require mothers and fathers to care for their children, but no loving parent ever thinks of those laws! Parents care for their children because they love them.

God wants obedience *from the heart*. It is this truth that underlies the Book of Deuteronomy. The word means "second law," since in Deuteronomy Moses repeats the law for the new generation about to enter Canaan. But Deuteronomy is

different from Exodus, because
Deuteronomy emphasizes *the heart*. The
word *love* is introduced in this book,
because love is the motive for obeying the
law. In Exodus, the emphasis is on
judgment and fear; but in Deuteronomy
the emphasis is on blessing and love. Of
course, there are in this book warnings
against sin; but the main theme is love.

Why did God choose Israel? "Because
He loved your fathers, therefore He chose
their descendants after them"
(Deuteronomy 4:37).

What is Israel's confession of faith?
"Hear, O Israel! The Lord is our God, the
Lord is one! And you shall love the Lord
your God with all your heart and with all
your soul and with all your might"
(Deuteronomy 6:4, 5).

Is Israel better than any other nation?
"The Lord did not set His love on you nor
choose you because you were more in
number than any of the peoples, for you
were the fewest of all peoples, but because
the Lord loved you and kept the oath
which He swore to your forefathers . . ."
(Deuteronomy 7:7, 8).

What does God require of his people?
"And now, Israel, what does the Lord your
God require from you, but to fear the
Lord your God, to walk in all His ways
and love Him, and to serve the Lord your
God with all your heart and with all your

soul" (Deuteronomy 10:12). "You shall therefore love the Lord your God, and always keep His charge . . ." (Deuteronomy 11:1).

But is it not enough that Israel is circumcised? "Moreover the Lord your God will circumcise your heart and the heart of your descendants, to love the Lord your God with all your heart and with all your soul, in order that you may live" (Deuteronomy 30:6).

Moses makes it clear to Israel—and to us—that the secret of obeying is loving. It is no wonder that Deuteronomy was our Lord's favorite book when he was here on earth. He quoted from it more than from any other. In the entire New Testament, Deuteronomy is quoted or referred to over eighty times. It is the book of loving obedience and obedient love.

C You and I cannot command others to love us, yet God commands us to love him! He has the right to command us because he always must will for us that which is the highest and the best. Furthermore, "God's commandments are God's enablements." By his very commanding, he assures us that this love is possible. Of ourselves, we cannot love him. "Apart from Me you can do nothing" (John 15:5). But "I can do all

things through Him who strengthens me"
(Philippians 4:13).

It is possible for us to love him, and to
love him more and more. And the more
we love him, the more we will obey him.
The more we obey him, the more we will
abide in him. And the more we abide in
him, the more we will bear fruit. And the
more we bear fruit, *the more we will live!*

There is a secret to loving.

Secret One
The secret
of living
is fruitbearing.

Secret Two
The secret
of fruitbearing
is abiding.

Secret Three
The secret
of abiding
is obeying.

Secret Four
The secret
of obeying
is loving.

Secret Five
The secret
of loving
is knowing.

*No longer do I call you
slaves; for the slave does
not know what his master
is doing; but I have
called you friends, for all
things that I have heard
from My Father I have
made known to you.*
(JOHN 15:15)

My hobby is reading biographies. I have hundreds of them in my library, and some of them I have read many times. There are a few famous preachers, for example, that interest me greatly, and I have every biography of them that I can find. The better I get to know them, the more I appreciate them.

However, I have biographies of a few great men (not preachers) whose lives utterly disgust me. The better I get to know them, the more I wish I had never heard of them!

Phillips Brooks used to say that "familiarity breeds contempt only with contemptible things or contemptible people." He is right. I cannot conceive of familiarity breeding contempt in the lives of a loving husband and wife who have shared a home for fifty years. At most golden wedding anniversary celebrations, the couple usually says, "We know each other better today than ever before, and we love each other more!"

The better you know Jesus Christ, the more you will love him. Your first knowledge of Jesus Christ was in connection with your salvation. "And this is eternal life, that they may know Thee the only true God, and Jesus Christ whom Thou hast sent" (John 17:3). But salvation is only the beginning. It is our privilege and joy to "grow in the grace and knowledge of our Lord and Savior Jesus Christ" (2 Peter 3:18). The Apostle Paul had been a Christian at least twenty-five years when he wrote to the church at Philippi, "That I may know Him" (Philippians 3:10). And Paul had visited the third heaven!

Why is it important for us to get to know Christ better? For one thing, salvation is a living relationship, and we cannot grow as Christians apart from personal fellowship with the Savior. It is easy for us to substitute other things—even good things—for this personal fellowship with Christ. We must beware of a second-hand relationship. Every book we read, every meeting we attend, every spiritual contact we make must in some way add to our personal knowledge of Jesus Christ. The better we get to know him, the more we grow in the Christian life and experience maturity.

But something else is true: the better we know him, the more we become like him. Just as two friends gradually become alike, or a husband and wife gradually grow together, so the believer and the Savior grow together as they fellowship with each

other. Moses met God on the mountaintop
and came down with the glory on his face,
a glory that faded away. We have Christ
living within; and as we commune with
him, his glory radiates through us. God's
purpose for our lives is that we might be
"conformed to the image of His Son"
(Romans 8:29). Of course, when Jesus
Christ returns, we shall be like him
(1 John 3:1, 2); but we can start becoming
like him today. The better you get to know
him, the more you become like him.

There is a third result of knowing Christ
better: you get to know yourself better,
and you become your best self. Learning
more about Jesus Christ does not make
you less of a person; rather, it brings out
of you all that God has put in you for his
glory. The amazing thing about the
Christian life is that we Christians all seek
to be more like Christ, yet we are not
imitating one another! Becoming like
Christ is a process that helps us become
ourselves and fulfill the purposes God has
for us. Each of the twelve apostles was
different, yet each of them accomplished
God's will in his own assigned way.

So, getting to know Christ better leads to
spiritual growth, which makes us more like
Christ and helps us become all that he
wants us to become. But there is another
wonderful result of growing in your
knowledge of Christ: *the better you know him,*

the more you love him. The secret of obeying is loving, and the secret of loving is knowing.

Jesus Christ wants us to know him better. This is why he calls us "friends" and not "slaves." No master stoops to explain his plans to a slave; but a friend shares his heart and mind with those who are dear to him. The word that Jesus uses for "friends" is used in Greek literature for "an intimate at court." We are friends of the King! He wants to share himself and his plans with us.

As you read the Gospel records in the New Testament, you see how patiently and lovingly our Lord revealed himself and his plans to his disciples. At times the disciples were disgustingly ignorant and almost unteachable. Often he had to bring them to the end of themselves before they were willing to listen and learn. Jesus knew just how much they could take and when they were ready for a new lesson. "I have many more things to say to you, but you cannot bear them now" (John 16:12).

Because he is our Friend, we can go to him, talk with him, and listen to him. Christ wants to share with us all that he has heard from the Father. This he does through his Word, by his Spirit. "But when

He, the Spirit of truth, comes, He will guide you into all the truth . . ." (John 16:13). As you read the Word, meditate on it, pray over it, and ask the Spirit to guide you, then you get to know Christ better.

No matter where you turn in the Word, you meet Jesus Christ. "And beginning with Moses and with all the prophets, He explained to them the things concerning Himself in all the Scriptures" (Luke 24:27). He is seen in type and prophecy in the Old Testament. He is seen ministering on earth in the Gospels, and ministering through his church in the Book of Acts. The epistles interpret for us the spiritual truths contained in the Person and work of Christ. The Book of the Revelation depicts him as the slain Lamb, the Judge, and the King of Kings. The theme of the whole Bible is Jesus Christ, the Son of God.

One of the benefits of Christian fellowship is the opportunity for others to help us learn more about Christ. Believers who have walked with him longer than we have can tell us much about the Savior and his gracious working in their lives. We, in turn, can encourage others with our own witness. Where even two or three believers are gathered in his name, he is there to reveal himself.

As we grow spiritually, we also see him in nature and history as well as in the Word. To be sure, the Bible is the primary source of spiritual knowledge about God; but it is still true that "The heavens are telling of the glory of God" (Psalm 19:1). When he was here on earth, Jesus saw the hand of God in the lilies and the birds. He took the common things of life, like water, bread, seed, and even children, and from them taught profound lessons about God. When you have the Word of God in your heart, you can look at creation and see the hand of God at work.

So, the better you know Christ, the more you will love him. When you begin to understand the glory of his person and the wonder of his work, you will worship and adore him. He will become the preeminent one in your life. Your love for him will not obliterate your love for others: it will sanctify your love and enrich it. We must not love our family, for example, more than we love Christ; but the more we love Christ, the more love we will show to our family *to the glory of God.* As your love for Christ grows, your love for others will be purified; the selfishness will be taken away.

But the more you love Christ, the more you will obey him. And the more you obey him, the more you will abide in him. As you abide in him, you will bear fruit; and the more you bear fruit, *the more you will live!*

It all begins with your knowing Christ in a deeper way, because the secret of loving is knowing.

I urge you therefore, brethren, by the mercies of God, to present your bodies a living and holy sacrifice, acceptable to God, which is your spiritual service of worship.
And do not be conformed to this world, but be transformed by the renewing of your mind, that you may prove what the will of God is, that which is good and acceptable and perfect.
(ROMANS *12:1, 2*)

Down through the centuries, men and women of God have made an important discovery. They have discovered that, if they are going to be fruitful for the Lord, they must spend time with him each day. Some Christians call this their "Quiet Time"; others know it as "personal devotions." No matter what name you give it, the experience is an important one.

When our Lord was ministering on earth, he started each day with this kind of fellowship with his Father. "And in the early morning, while it was still dark, He arose and went out and departed to a lonely place, and was praying there" (Mark 1:35). The Messianic passage in Isaiah 50 gives us some insight into what Jesus did.

"He awakens Me morning by morning,
He awakens My ear to listen as a disciple"
(Isaiah 50:4). Jesus spent the early hours
of the day talking to his Father and
listening to his Father.

Successful Christians of all ages have
learned that secret. If you start your day
with the Lord, you may abide in him all
day and experience the joy of bearing
fruit. It demands discipline, to be sure; but
it is the kind of discipline that becomes a
spiritual dynamic.

If you want to know Christ better, abide
in him, and enjoy a fruitful life, then
determine to have a disciplined and
satisfying devotional life.

What are the elements involved in such
a life? They are given to us in Romans
12:1, 2, the verses quoted at the beginning
of this chapter.

1. *Give God your body.* When you first
awaken in the morning, simply give your
body to God—*and then get up!* Like the
soldier hearing reveille, get up! Selfish
indulgence of the body often leads to
sinful indifference later in the day. Follow
the example of Paul who said, "And
everyone who competes in the games
exercises self-control in all things . . . but I
buffet my body and make it my slave . . ."

(1 Corinthians 9:25, 27). God wants to use your body to bear fruit for his glory. He wants his life to work in and through your body. By faith, give him your body as your first step in worship each day.

2. *Give God your mind.* He wants to transform you by renewing your mind. How does he do this? *Through his Word.* Reach for your Bible, read it, and let the Spirit of God teach you. Where should you read in your Bible? I suggest that you adopt a plan for reading through the Bible. I like to start in Genesis 1, Psalm 1, and Matthew 1, and keep reading. I do not always read three chapters a day. Sometimes God stops me at one verse! But you will want to have a systematic plan for reading through the Bible. Do not try to do it in any given time; let the Lord set the pace for you.

Meditation is to the heart and mind what digestion is to the body. Some people read the Bible the way they read a cook book, and you can starve that way! Take time to let the Spirit reveal Christ to you in the Word. The Holy Spirit is your teacher. If you yield to him and ask for his help, he will open the Word to you. When you learn a spiritual truth, receive it into your inner self. Make it a part of your "spiritual muscles." As the Lord gradually changes and transforms your mind, you will know Christ better and love him more.

3. *Give God your will.* ". . . that you may prove what the will of God is . . ." (Romans 12:2). How do you give God your will? *Through prayer.* As you pray, you yield your will to God. You tell him that he can do in and through you whatever he knows is best. Prayer involves many things: confessing sin, asking for God's help, interceding for others. But basically, prayer is saying, "Yet not as I will, but as Thou wilt" (Matthew 26:39).

Many people have found it helpful to have a prayer list. It helps them remember their requests. I like to keep several prayer lists, in fact, one for each day of the week. This keeps me from praying for the same things in a ritual way each day. It also enables me to pray about more needs and more people. There are some items that I remember each day, and the Lord always brings new requests to my attention as I pray. Whatever approach you use, be systematic in your praying; and it will not hurt to keep a record of the way God has answered.

4. *Give God your heart.* Worship him. Love him. Be silent before him in your love. Do not try to manufacture a "spiritual feeling." We worship God "in spirit and truth" (John 4:24). A friend and I were taking a long trip together, and for many miles we said nothing to each other. Then my friend said, "You know,

it's good to have the kind of relationship that isn't shattered by silence!" Often, as my wife and I drive together, we say nothing; and then when we do speak, we find we are thinking about the same things. You can have a similar relationship with the Lord as you worship him and love him from your heart.

These are the elements involved in a satisfying devotional life: each morning give God your body, mind, will, and heart.

You can see how these four elements work together with the five secrets I have been sharing with you. The secret of living is fruitbearing, and the secret of fruitbearing is abiding.

What is the secret of abiding? It is *obeying:* give God *your will.*

What is the secret of obeying? It is *loving:* give God *your heart.*

What is the secret of loving? It is *knowing:* give God *your mind.*

In other words, when you surrender heart, mind, and will to God each day, you are able to abide in him and draw upon his spiritual power. When you yield him your body, he can work through you to produce the spiritual fruit that he wants you to bear. Instead of being "conformed to this world," you are *transformed* by his power—and you glorify his name.

I cannot emphasize too much the importance of this daily quiet time with the

Lord. But I must add that meeting God in the morning also means that you fellowship with him all day long. At different times during the day, you will find the Holy Spirit speaking to you. *Listen!* There will be occasions when your heart will reach out for God. *Pause and love him!* It is as you abide in him all day long that he is able to work in and through you. This is how you bear fruit.

Catch the foxes for us,
The little foxes that are ruining the vineyards.
(SONG OF SOLOMON 2:15)

As you begin to abide in Christ and become a fruitful branch, you must watch out for enemies. If you do not, you will begin to lose your fruitfulness.

As the Vinedresser, your Father wants to keep the branches clean. Dirty branches and leaves can hinder fruitfulness. The Father keeps you clean through his Word. "You are already clean because of the word which I have spoken to you" (John 15:3). In the Bible, water for drinking is a picture of the Holy Spirit (John 7:37-39); but water for washing is a picture of God's Word. As you read his Word, it reveals your heart; it cleanses your mind. If God shows you some uncleanness, you can

confess it and receive his promised
forgiveness (1 John 1:9).

Along with dirt, there are insects and
diseases that can bring blight and even
death. These the Father must remove.
Sometimes he must cut away a diseased
part in order to spare the healthy parts.
You and I may not enjoy this surgery, but
it is good for us. It has well been said that
the Father is never so near to the branch
as when he is pruning it. He may hurt us,
but he will never harm us.

The "little foxes" can also ruin the
vineyard. Foxes usually feed on small
animals, but they also eat fruit. They are
not too careful in the way they steal the
fruit, and thus they damage the branches.
In the Christian life, it is usually the little
things that rob us of blessing. It is not
necessary for a herd of cattle to trample
the vineyard, or a fire to burn it. The
"little foxes" can destroy it, if only given
enough time.

Take, for example, some of the "little
sins" that we fail to deal with: impatience,
criticism, short temper, fussiness,
questionable humor. These may be "faults"
or "sins in good standing" in the eyes of
men, but what are they in the eyes of
God? It seemed a little thing for King
David to leave the battlefield and return to
the palace for a rest; but that little bit of
indulgence led him into adultery and

murder. It was just a "little nap" that Peter took in the garden, but his lack of watching and praying led to his shameful denials of Christ.

The little foxes spoil the vines, so watch for them *and kill them!* Name the sins, confess them, and ask for God's forgiveness. Never feed a "little fox." He will grow up and devour you!

It takes diligence and dedication to bear fruit for God. Once we become lazy and careless, we cease to bear fruit. Solomon paints a meaningful picture of this truth in Proverbs 24:30-34.

> *I passed by the field of the sluggard,*
> *And by the vineyard of the man lacking*
>   *sense;*
> *And behold, it was completely*
>   *overgrown with thistles,*
> *Its surface was covered with nettles,*
> *And its stone wall was broken down.*
> *When I saw, I reflected upon it;*
> *I looked, and received instruction.*
> *"A little sleep, a little slumber,*
> *A little folding of the hands to rest."*
> *Then your poverty will come as a*
>   *robber,*
> *And your want like an armed man.*

"A little sleep—a little slumber."

"The little foxes that are ruining the vineyards."

Deal with sin while it is little! Otherwise, it will grow and do great damage, and rob you of your fruitfulness.

Too much self-analysis and introspection is not good. But it is good for us to search our hearts and confess our sins to God. It is good to uncover the "little foxes" before they destroy us. "Let us cleanse ourselves from all defilement of flesh and spirit, perfecting holiness in the fear of God" (2 Corinthians 7:1).

And another angel, the one who has power over fire, came out from the altar; and he called with a loud voice to him who had the sharp sickle, saying, "Put in your sharp sickle, and gather the clusters from the vine of the earth, because her grapes are ripe."

And the angel swung his sickle to the earth, and gathered the clusters from the vine of the earth, and threw them into the great wine press of the wrath of God. (REVELATION 14:18, 19)

"The vine of the earth!"

This is God's description of society without Christ. Those who have trusted Christ are branches in the Vine of heaven. Those who have rejected him are branches in the vine of the earth.

And they are destined for judgment.

This present world system looks fruitful and successful. Unbelievers tell us that "things are getting better and better." But God sees the "vine of the earth" ripening for his wrath. The clusters will be cut off and the fruit cast into the winepress of the wrath of God.

If you have trusted Christ as your Savior, then you do not belong to this "vine of the earth." You are a branch in the true Vine from heaven.

If you have never trusted Christ, then you are a part of the "vine of the earth," and you are destined for judgment.

BUT—you can escape that judgment!

Listen to God's good news for you.

"For God so loved the world, that He gave His only begotten Son, that whoever believes in Him should not perish, but have eternal life" (John 3:16).

WHOEVER—that includes you.

BELIEVES—that also includes you.

Trust Christ! Yield yourself to him!

Today, abandon the "vine of the earth" and, by faith, become a branch in the true Vine. Start living! Start bearing fruit for God's glory!

"Whoever will call upon the name of the Lord will be saved" (Romans 10:13).